AF846095

276794

The University of Huddersfield Library
Queensgate, Huddersfield. HD1 3DH

Telephone: Office hours: 422288 Extn. 2045
Evenings: 421800

Class No: 347

Suffix: JASON-LLOYD

This book is to be returned on or
before the last date stamped below

RETURNED
18 DEC 1998

RETURNED

RETURNED

5 OCT 2001
RETURNED

16 JUL 2002
RETURNED

Titles in the Legal Framework Series

The Legal Framework of the Constitution
Leonard Jason-Lloyd

The Framework of Criminal Law
Leonard Jason-Lloyd

The Framework of the English Legal System
Leonard Jason-Lloyd

The Legal Framework of the European Union
Leonard Jason-Lloyd and Sukhwinder Bajwa

The Legal Framework of the Modern Company
Leonard Jason-Lloyd and Larry Mead

The Legal Framework of Police Powers
Leonard Jason-Lloyd

The Framework of

The English Legal System

Leonard Jason-Lloyd

Lecturer in Law, University of Derby, and visiting Lecturer in Law at the Midlands Centre for Criminology and Criminal Justice, Loughborough University and the Scarman Centre for the Study of Public Order at the University of Leicester

FRANK CASS

LONDON • PORTLAND, OR.

UNIVERSITY
LIBRARY
14 MAY 1998
04814266
HUDDERSFIELD

Published in 1997 in Great Britain by
FRANK CASS & CO. LTD.
Newbury House, 900 Eastern Avenue,
London IG2 7HH, England

and in the United States of America by
FRANK CASS
c/o ISBS
5804 N.E. Hassalo Street
Portland, Oregon 97213-3644

Copyright © 1996 Frank Cass & Co. Ltd.

British Library Cataloguing in Publication Data

Jason-Lloyd, Leonard
The framework of the English legal system
1. Procedure (Law) – England 2. Law – England
I. Title II. The English legal system
344.2'07

ISBN 0 7146 4776 4 (cloth)
ISBN 0 7146 4287 8 (paper)
ISSN 0965 3473

Library of Congress Cataloging-in-Publication Data

Jason-Lloyd, Leonard, 1945-
The framework of the English legal system / Leonard Jason-Lloyd.
p. cm. – (Legal framework series, ISSN 0965-3473)
Includes bibliographical references and index.
ISBN 0 7146 4776 4 (cloth) ISBN 0 7146-4287-8 (paper)
1. Law–Great Britain. I. Title. II. Series
KD662.J37 1996
349.42–dc20
[344.2] 96-28520
CIP

All rights reserved. No part of this publication may be reproduced in any form or by any means, electronic, mechanical, photocopying, recording or otherwise, without the prior permission of Frank Cass and Company Limited.

Printed in Great Britain by
Cromwell Press Ltd., Melksham, Wilts.

Contents

1

The Historical Development of the English Courts

The basic origins of the present English legal system can be traced back to the Norman conquest in 1066. Prior to the invasion by William I of Normandy, England had a very fragmented system of justice which was often primitive and difficult to obtain. The Anglo-Saxon courts were sometimes characterised by such practices as trial by ordeal, where the accused had to take hold of a red-hot iron and his guilt or innocence was determined by the extent of the blistering. In contrast to the relatively weak control exerted over the realm by the Anglo-Saxon kings, the early Norman monarchs established strong central government and this subsequently led to the evolution of a more efficient system of justice.

It was during the reign of Henry II that the first circuit judges were established. These were Royal judges who had both civil and criminal jurisdiction and travelled England within a system of circuits devised by the King. These early justices, who were usually noblemen or high-ranking priests, would return to Westminster at the end of each round of travels and compare notes on the local customs and traditions encountered while on circuit. They would then agree on the best of these and gradually a uniform set of legal rules evolved. This was the beginning of the common law of England. The doctrine of precedent also began to develop in which earlier judgments formulated in the courts were adhered to in later decisions thus making the law more certain.

Apart from the circuit judges the central government also performed a judicial role. This body was the King's Council (known as the *Curia Regis*) and under Henry I they presided over the development of the Court of the Exchequer which, as the name denotes, dealt primarily with taxation disputes. Other courts developed, such as the Court of Common Pleas which was operated by the circuit judges exclusively for civil cases. This court remained intact until 1873 reflecting not only its popularity but also the general continuity of the development of the English legal system. This continuity is exemplified even further by the Court of the King's Bench in which medieval kings sometimes sat in judgment and which still exists today as a part of the High Court.

Concurrent with all these early developments was a major problem inherent within the civil law. Proceedings could only be started by a writ obtainable from the Chancery and, although available for each remedy, they were written in standard worded form. If a case differed from that covered by the wording of a writ, even slightly, no remedy was available. As a consequence litigants falling under this category began to petition the King to personally do justice. The numbers increased to the extent that the reigning monarchs delegated this task to their Chancellors and eventually their own court emerged, namely the Court of Chancery. The main feature of this court was that it dispensed justice in the form of equity (fairness) and this system effectively bridged the gaps left by the common law courts. Equity judgments were based largely upon the conscience of the Chancellors who in the early days were priests and as a result their court became very popular.

Rivalry thus ensued between the Court of Chancery and the common law courts which persisted until matters came to a head as a result of the *Earl of Oxford's Case (1616)*. In this case the Chancellor went against the judgment of the Chief Justice of the common law courts. Acting upon the advice of his Attorney-General, James I ruled that in future, whenever the two forms of law were in conflict, equity must prevail. Equity was not always popular, however. Sometimes its initial flexibility deteriorated into uncertainty with successive Chancellors making unpredictable judgments. By the beginning of the nineteenth century a system of precedent was established in order to obviate this problem but this became almost as rigid as the common law. Furthermore, the Court of Chancery became notorious for long delays and subsequent high costs. During the early nineteenth century one Lord Chancellor presided over a case that lasted ten years!

A major cornerstone in English legal history was the passing of the Judicature Acts (1873–75). This included the instituting of the Supreme Court of Judicature which contained the Court of Appeal and the High Court of Justice, which in turn included the Chancery Division, Common Pleas Division, Exchequer Division, Queen's Bench Division and the Probate, Divorce and Admiralty Division. (The latter court was described by one commentator as a curious conglomeration of wives, wills and wrecks!) The Judicature Acts both rationalised the court system and amalgamated the common law and equity so that both forms of justice could be dispensed in any court concurrently. Further rationalisation took place in 1881 resulting in three divisions of the High Court remaining, namely the Queen's Bench Division, the Chancery Division and the Probate, Divorce and Admiralty Division. This structure remained until 1970 when further major changes were effected resulting in the present system which will be described in subsequent chapters.

2

The Criminal Courts

As discussed in the previous chapter, the English legal system is the result of over 900 years continuous development which makes it unique among other nations. Inevitably, this has created a structure that is both complicated and at times anomalous. It is, therefore, essential that constant reference is made to the portrayal of the existing court structure as illustrated in Figure 1 throughout the study of subsequent chapters.

Before describing the courts of criminal jurisdiction it is important to mention that criminal offences fall into three categories, namely summary, indictable and those which are triable either way.

SUMMARY OFFENCES

Crimes under this heading constitute the more minor offences which statute (Act of Parliament) stipulates must be dealt with exclusively by the magistrates' courts. This is primarily intended to prevent the higher courts being overloaded with relatively trivial cases. Offences of this nature include the vast majority of motoring offences, common assault, dropping litter, obstructing the highway, interfering with a motor vehicle, kerb crawling, supplying solvent for intoxication, being drunk and disorderly, and many more.

INDICTABLE OFFENCES

Crimes committed within this category are the more serious and sometimes the gravest of all offences against society. These tend to be the cases more commonly brought to public attention, such as murder, rape, arson, armed robbery, kidnapping, serious fraud, and a host of others. All offences under this heading must be tried in the Crown Court and receive sentence there.

OFFENCES TRIABLE EITHER WAY

This is a descriptive term which indicates that offences under this heading can either be relatively minor or quite serious. Therefore, subject to the general approval of the magistrates and the defendant, they may be tried either in the magistrates' or the Crown Court. These offences include burglary, violent disorder, theft, affray, handling stolen goods, gross indecency, assault occasioning actual bodily harm and possession of a controlled drug, to name but a few. Crimes which fall under this category are also stipulated in statute.

THE MAGISTRATES' COURTS – THEIR CRIMINAL JURISDICTION

There are approximately 700 magistrates' courts in England and Wales. These are usually very busy courts, borne out by the fact that they deal with about two million cases a year which includes approximately 97 per cent of all criminal cases. Despite their relatively limited sentencing powers, magistrates' courts fulfil a vital role within the criminal justice system since they are widely acknowledged to be quick, efficient and comparatively inexpensive. Furthermore, they also perform important functions under civil law which will be discussed later.

The Magistrates

In this country, we have a truly unique feature within our administration of justice whereby about 30,000 persons dispense justice on a non-professional, unpaid, part-time basis. Yet it is a system which generally works well. Lay magistrates are not legally qualified but receive some basic training covering such matters as court procedures, the examination of pre-sentence reports and available penalties for certain offences. However, with regard to the finer points on court powers and procedures, including the application of the law to certain facts, lay magistrates rely upon the clerk of the court who usually sits directly in front of them and is either a qualified solicitor or barrister. The clerks must not participate in the actual judgments – this is a role solely exercised by the magistrates.

Serving members of the lay magistracy are entitled to use the letters 'JP' after their names meaning that they are a Justice of the Peace, an ancient title that originated several centuries ago.

As mentioned earlier, JPs serve in a part-time capacity. The time they are able to devote to duties on the Bench often depends on other commitments including their paid occupation but usually the minimum time spent as a JP in court is 26 sittings a year, one sitting constituting a half-day. Furthermore, they do not receive payment for their services – only reimbursement of expenses and any loss of earnings. Lay magistrates usually sit in groups of three, although if necessary two may be allowed to conduct proceedings. The more senior magistrate sits in the middle and generally plays the leading role. It is common practice that they should not all be of the same sex.

The selection and composition of lay magistrates has given rise to some comment in recent years. A number of commentators have drawn attention to the general lack of certain elements of modern society within the lay magistracy. For instance, there is a marked absence of younger people or those from the working classes since most lay magistrates tend to come from the professional or managerial occupational sectors and are often middle-aged. The predominance of people from these backgrounds does not point to a deliberate attempt to preclude other sections of the community. The problem lies mainly in the difficulties associated with lower-paid occupations, as, for example, obtaining leave of absence for attendance at court. Some of the problems associated with lay justices have been solved to a certain extent by using stipendiary magistrates who are usually to be found in the busier inner-city courts. These are qualified barristers or solicitors with at least five years' experience who are paid a salary for their duties and therefore perform their tasks on a full-time basis. Stipendiary magistrates usually sit alone in court. The Chief Metropolitan Magistrate, who is the country's most senior stipendiary, sits in the most famous court of summary jurisdiction, namely Bow Street Magistrates' Court. It is generally he who considers extradition requests by foreign states.

The Functions of Magistrates' Courts

Apart from their civil jurisdiction which will be discussed later, magistrates' courts perform a vital function within the criminal justice system since nearly all criminal cases are brought before them initially even if they are referred elsewhere. Summary offences are dealt with in their entirety by the magistrates and generally the only time they may come into contact with a higher court is if there is an appeal. A very large proportion of defendants plead guilty (where minor motoring and certain other offences are concerned, this can be done by letter), in which case the justices only have to consider the penalty. Those who plead not guilty are usually given an adjournment of several weeks to arrange for their defence. A summary trial then takes place in the magistrates' court where witnesses are examined and cross-examined. This is followed by the judgment and, if found guilty, sentence is then pronounced. There are no juries in the magistrates' courts, therefore only the justices decide on the guilt or innocence of the defendant in addition to the penalty, where applicable.

When an indictable offence has been committed the defendant is initially brought before the magistrates where his name and address is confirmed and the charge read out. He is not required to state whether he is guilty or not guilty at that stage. The case will then be referred to the Crown Court following a procedure called 'committal proceedings',[1] which is largely an examination of the case papers by a magistrate prior to the defendant's committal to the Crown Court. This process replaces the earlier 'committal proceedings' which sometimes took the form of mini-trials. These are being abolished by the Criminal Procedure & Investigations Act 1996 in favour of the quicker and less costly new-style proceedings which generally concentrate on written submissions rather than oral argument. The purpose of this procedure is to act as a filter in order to ensure that only those cases where the prosecution's evidence is sufficiently strong will actually go before the Crown Court. Where this is not so, the proceedings can be discontinued since there will be no case to answer.

Offences triable either way may be dealt with in one of the following ways. The defendant may decide to plead not guilty but request that the actual trial takes place in the magistrates' court. If the justices agree to a summary trial, this will take place following an adjournment. If found guilty, the defendant will be sentenced by the magistrates but if the nature of the crime is more serious than was immediately apparent, they may send the defendant to the Crown Court to be sentenced. If the defendant pleads guilty, however, the magistrates may either sentence the offender, or if the nature of the offence is serious, they may refer the case to the Crown Court for sentence if it falls outside the scope of their powers. If the magistrates refuse to try such a case summarily, or if the defendant wishes to be tried

1. The new-style committal proceedings are due to be implemented possibly during early 1997.

before a jury, the case must then be committed to the Crown Court via committal proceedings.[2] The diagram in Figure 2 illustrates the various routes taken by criminal cases when passing into the magistrates' courts system.

It is important to mention that between these various stages the cases are adjourned. As mentioned earlier, one of the reasons is to enable the defendant to make preparations for their defence, but another major reason is to enable the justices to obtain information about the defendant prior to sentencing. This includes medical and pre-sentence reports which may assist the justices in deciding the most appropriate penalty or disposal. The adjournments will entail the defendant either being released on bail or remanded in custody. If the defendant is released on bail, there may sometimes be conditions attached to their remaining at liberty, such as reporting to their local police station at regular intervals or not going to certain places or near specific individuals. They may also be required to live at a certain address such as a bail hostel and a curfew may even be imposed. These provisions usually apply to more serious offences, particularly when crimes of violence have been committed. This is known as 'conditional bail', but in most cases where bail is granted there are no conditions attached other than the requirement that the defendant attends court when requested, hence the term 'unconditional bail'. Sometimes the offence, or the way it was committed, are so serious that the

2. Under the Criminal Procedure and Investigations Act 1996, defendants charged with triable either way offences will be invited to indicate their intention to plead guilty or not guilty, before magistrates decide whether they are willing to try the case summarily.

court will not grant bail. This also applies if the defendant has a record of absconding once granted bail or has to be remanded in custody for his own safety. In such instances the defendant will be sent to a remand centre or the remand wing of a prison until his/her next date of appearance. Magistrates also have to deal with defendants who either appear to be or who are suffering from mental disorders and it is necessary to remand them to a hospital in order to obtain medical reports, or pass an appropriate disposal option under the Mental Health Act 1983, such as a hospital order.

Since the beginning of 1986 a further responsibility has been incumbent upon magistrates, namely decisions on whether to authorise the police to continue holding suspects detained without charge. Justices can authorise the police to hold suspects for up to a further 60 hours beyond the maximum time the police are allowed to detain an arrested person for questioning without charge. However, this only applies to serious arrestable offences which are normally the most serious crimes.

Magistrates' Sentencing Powers

Although there are specific limitations on the sentencing powers of magistrates, a wide variety of criminal sanctions are still available to them. (See Figure 3 which depicts the criminal sanctions available to all the courts of criminal jurisdiction.) The most severe penalty which can be imposed by magistrates is imprisonment (or detention in a young offender institution if the offender is under 21), although their power to impose a custodial sentence is limited to a maximum of six months per offence where appropriate.

However, they can combine this maximum for two offences triable either way to run consecutively, thereby making a total custodial sentence of one year. In exceptional circumstances, a prison sentence (but not detention in a young offender institution) may be suspended.

As an alternative to custody, a number of community sentences are available to magistrates, namely probation, community service, combination orders, attendance centre orders, supervision orders and curfew orders. Probation orders may exist in simple form, usually requiring regular visits to a probation officer plus a few other formalities, or special conditions may be attached to such an order. These may include the requirement to attend drug or alcohol rehabilitation courses or to receive psychiatric treatment either as an in-patient or out-patient.

Community service orders require the offender to perform up to 240 hours work in the community. If an element of supervision is also required, then a combination order will be passed as a sentence which is basically community service and probation mixed in a certain composite. Attendance centre orders can be imposed on offenders up to the age of 20 inclusive, and require the offender to attend a specified place for usually a few hours at a time in order to keep them away from certain venues where they have committed an offence (for example, football matches).

Curfew orders are a comparatively new sentence, although the imposition of curfews has long been a part of other powers held by the courts of criminal jurisdiction, such as a condition of bail. As a sentence, the imposition of a curfew order requires the offender to remain at home for several hours per day or night and this may be enforced by the offender wearing an electronic monitoring device around his wrist or ankle. If he leaves his home or interferes with the device, this will be picked-up by a local monitoring station and the offender could be returned to the court to face breach proceedings. Finally, supervision orders, which are broadly the equivalent of probation for young offenders, are usually given by magistrates sitting in the Youth Court which will be discussed below.

The most widely used of all the criminal sanctions is the imposition of fines. Generally, the maximum fine that magistrates can impose is £5,000, although an important factor that has to be taken into account is the offender's ability to pay in addition to the seriousness of the offence. However, other financial penalties may be imposed where appropriate such as compensation orders. Particularly where property is damaged or where injury has been caused, magistrates frequently require the offender to compensate the victim of the crime for financial loss or personal distress. Deprivation of offenders' property may also be imposed in appropriate cases, namely forfeiture, restitution and confiscation orders, although the latter is limited in magistrates' courts to a few specified summary offences.

The least punitive of all the sentences that can be meted out by magistrates are conditional and absolute discharges. An absolute discharge means that the offender receives no punishment for the offence and only acknowledges that an offence has been committed. This usually applies where the offence is purely technical or very trivial. A conditional discharge also imposes no immediate penalty on conviction, but this will be activated if the offender re-offends within a stated period of time and will be added to the penalty for the latest offence.

Finally, magistrates have the power to bind persons

over to keep the peace and/or be of good behaviour. This is regarded as preventative justice and is sometimes used in cases involving minor assaults or less serious public order offences. In such cases, magistrates will require the offender not to break the law within a certain period of time (usually one year) and will state a sum of money which will be forfeited in the event of a breach. This sum of money is known as a 'recognisance'. Dealing with breaches of the peace in this way is an ancient power held by justices of the peace since 1361, although it exists in more modern form under the Magistrates' Courts Act 1980.

Appeals from Magistrates' Courts

Appeals against guilty verdicts or sentences imposed by magistrates' courts go to the Crown Court. These procedures are covered in the final part of this chapter under the heading of the appellate functions of the Crown Court. If an interpretation of the law is disputed, appeals will be directed to the Queen's Bench Division of the High Court by way of 'case stated'. In exceptional cases the appeal will then go direct to the House of Lords under the 'leap-frog' procedure. If purely procedure-related matters are disputed, such as magistrates exceeding their jurisdiction, or if there is a reasonable suspicion of bias in a particular case, an application for judicial review may be made to the Queen's Bench Division of the High Court, where one or more of the prerogative orders may be available (see Chapter 3).

The Youth Court

Magistrates with special training and ability in dealing with young people sit in the Youth Court (known as the 'juvenile court' prior to the Criminal Justice Act 1991), and these are responsible for dealing exclusively with children and young persons between the ages of ten to 17 inclusive who have committed criminal offences. Anyone below the age of ten is under the age of criminal responsibility, therefore they cannot be guilty of an offence. The Youth Court is less formal than its adult counterpart and proceedings are conducted largely in private. The sentencing powers of magistrates in the Youth Court differ slightly to those held in the adult section. For instance, a juvenile offender may be subject to a supervision order (the juvenile equivalent of probation) to which conditions may be attached, such as the requirement to have psychiatric treatment or the imposition of a night curfew. Custodial sentences may also be given, namely detention in a young offender institution for offenders aged 15 and above, or secure training orders for 12 to 14-year-olds inclusive which are due to be available soon. Fines, costs and compensation orders may also be made but the parents or guardians of young offenders are liable to pay if the juvenile is unable to meet the sum involved. This entails the Youth Court having to possess knowledge of the circumstances of both parents and the offender. Further penalties include the range of community sentences dependent upon the age of the offender (see Figure 3).

Under the Criminal Justice Act 1991, parents or guardians of young offenders under the age of 16 may be required to enter into a recognisance of up to £1,000 to prevent them from re-offending. Therefore, all or part of the recognisance could be forfeited if further offences are committed within three years or before the offender reaches the age of 18, whichever comes sooner. The Criminal Justice and Public Order Act 1994 goes further and provides that parents or guardian… offenders given a community sentence may be req… also to enter into a recognisance to ensure that the offender complies with the conditions of that sentence.

Appeals against decisions in the Youth Court take the same route as those from the magistrates' courts, namely to the Crown Court on matters affecting conviction or sentence, and to the Queen's Bench Division of the High Court on points of law by way of 'case stated' or applications for judicial review where appropriate.

Not every juvenile who commits a crime and is subsequently arrested automatically attends the Youth Court as a consequence. Many are officially cautioned by the police if it constitutes their first offence and the crime is not serious. This effectively diverts a large number away from the full panoply of the criminal justice system and avoids criminalising young people unnecessarily. There are occasions, however, when a juvenile may have to appear before an adult court. This applies when a juvenile commits an offence with an adult and consequently both must appear before the relevant courts that the adult would normally attend. Also, if a juvenile commits a 'grave' crime, which basically includes nearly all of the most serious offences which can attract 14 years' imprisonment or more if committed by an adult, or is involved in a homicide offence, the juvenile will be committed to the Crown Court.

The Crown Court

The Crown Court is the most popularised of all the English institutions exercising criminal jurisdiction, chiefly because the more serious crimes are tried there and the jury system is centred largely within this aspect of the administration of justice. As mentioned earlier, the more serious and gravest crimes are known as indictable offences. The term indictment is the formal written accusation of the alleged crime against the defendant. All indictable offences must be tried and sentenced in the Crown Court. If the alleged crime is one of those classed as triable either way then, by mutual agreement between the defendant and the justices, the case will be tried summarily in the magistrates' court. If found guilty, sentence will be pronounced by the magistrates unless the offence warrants a stiffer sentence in the Crown Court. However, if the defendant wishes to be tried before a jury or the justices do not agree to a summary trial, the case will be committed to the Crown Court for trial.

Crown Court Judges

Although the general term 'judge' is used to describe those who preside over Crown Court proceedings, there are three main categories of persons who occupy such positions. The most senior are High Court judges who usually hear only the most serious or contentious cases. They are dressed in scarlet robes and addressed as 'My Lord' or 'My Lady' in court. Then there are the circuit judges who generally hear the fairly serious offences. They are addressed as 'your Honour' and wear dark robes with violet edging and a red sash from shoulder to waist. The less serious offences are tried before judges who wear normal dark robes without any trimmings but are also addressed as 'your Honour'. These are Recorders (sometimes assistant or deputy recorders) who are barristers or occasionally solicitors who sit as part-time judges. Very often they are in the preparatory stages of becoming circuit judges.

There are six Crown Court circuits in England and Wales, namely:

North Eastern covering Newcastle, Teeside, Middlesbrough, York, Leeds, Bradford and Sheffield.

Northern covering Carlisle, Preston, Liverpool and Manchester.

Midland and Oxford, which includes Lincoln, Nottingham, Stafford, Warwick, Oxford, Leicester, Northampton and Birmingham.

Western, which includes Plymouth, Bodmin, Exeter, Bournemouth, Southampton, Portsmouth and Winchester.

South Eastern, covering London, Reading, Guildford, Brighton, Lewes, Chelmsford, Colchester, Cambridge, Ipswich and Norwich.

Wales and Chester, which covers all of Wales and also includes Chester.

Up to four experienced lay magistrates, who are used to assist in deciding appeals against conviction or sentence from the magistrates' courts due to their local knowledge and experience, may sit with the judge in the Crown Court. All judges sitting in the Crown Court have unlimited sentencing powers subject to the legal maximum for each offence. In practice, the most severe sentence available is life imprisonment which is mandatory for murder, but also constitutes the maximum discretionary sentence for such crimes as manslaughter, robbery, rape and arson. It is usual for a High Court judge to preside over cases likely to justify such penalties. There are also a variety of other penalties which are largely the same as those available to magistrates, such as suspended prison sentences, community sentences, deprivation of property, discharges and fines (although judges in certain circumstances can impose unlimited amounts in contrast to the general maximum of £5,000 in magistrates' courts).

Other Personnel

Clerks of the court are not usually legally qualified unlike their counterparts in magistrates' courts. This is because those who preside over Crown Court proceedings are judges who are well-qualified lawyers unlike lay magistrates who are not. Crown Court clerks are therefore generally in charge of its administration and the operation of its proceedings.

The Jury

Perhaps the most well-known characteristic of the Crown Court is the presence of 12 ordinary citizens called upon to judge the defendant. The jury system can be traced back at least 700 years and remains a vital component within the criminal justice system. Juries are selected from the electoral register and anyone between the ages of 18 and 70 is liable to be called for jury service. There are four main grounds upon which a person may not serve.

The first covers those who are *ineligible,* which includes persons engaged in work connected with the administration of justice such as practising or non-practising lawyers, members of the judiciary (including magistrates), prison and police officers, probation officers and staff working for the Crown Prosecution Service. Anyone who has worked in these occupations within ten years is also ineligible. Such persons are classed as ineligible to avoid bias and any conflict of interests. The clergy, monks and nuns are also ineligible, and ineligibility further extends to the mentally ill. It is an offence for a person to sit on a jury if they are ineligible.

The second category covers those who are *excused as of right,* namely occupational groups such as doctors, nurses, dentists, vets, firefighters, pharmacists, full-time members of Her Majesty's Armed Forces, as well as Members of Parliament and Peers in the House of Lords. Such persons are given automatic excusals as of right and such automatic excusals extend to other persons who may not necessarily work in essential services. These include individuals who have performed jury service within two years, persons more than 65 years old, and practising members of certain religious societies whose beliefs are incompatible with jury service.

The third grouping come under the heading of *miscellaneous or discretionary excusals.* These are individual cases of hardship covering such matters as dependent children or elderly relatives to look after, personal health problems, important business responsibilities, forthcoming examinations and booked holidays, and many more. However, excusals in these cases are at the discretion of the individual courts. In addition to compassionate considerations, this category of excusals includes persons with other good reasons for not serving on a jury, such as those who have some connection with the case.

Finally, there are those who are actually *disqualified* from serving on a jury. This includes those who have served any term of imprisonment, youth custody, community service or who have been given a suspended prison sentence within the previous ten years and also those placed on probation within the previous five years. Anyone who has been given a life sentence or the equivalent is disqualified for life, as is anyone given youth custody for five years or more. Also, anyone on either police or court bail may not serve on a jury. It is an offence for a person to sit on a jury if they are disqualified.

The prime function of the jury is to judge the guilt or innocence of the defendant. Prior to this decision the judge gives his or her summing-up which is a statement of the law as applied to the facts of the case.[3] The jury then retires to consider its verdict. In many cases a majority of ten out of 12 may be accepted if at least two hours has elapsed without a unanimous decision being made, although more time will usually be given in more serious or complex cases. If a jury cannot reach an agreement, then a retrial may be requested by the prosecution but this cannot occur more than once. Juries are not exclusive to the Crown Court. On rare occasions they are used in civil proceedings and even the Coroner's Court, which will be discussed later.

Lawyers in the Crown Court

Detailed analysis regarding the legal profession is given in a later chapter. Suffice to say at this juncture that there are two branches, namely solicitors and barristers, and it is still mainly the latter who play the leading role in the Crown Court through the examining and cross-examining of witnesses and generally advocating for one of the parties. The general role of the solicitors who are usually present in court is to advise

3. The Criminal Procedure and Investigations Act 1996 enables judges to order preparatory hearings in long or complex cases, where it is likely to assist the jury's understanding of a case.

the barristers (called counsel) on the conduct of the case, and to act as the liaison between their client and the barrister representing that client. Both sections of the legal profession may advocate in criminal proceedings in magistrates' courts and in recent years increasing numbers of solicitors approved by the Lord Chancellor have been given full rights of audience before the Crown Court, in accordance with his powers under the Courts and Legal Services Act 1990. However, for the time being the vast majority of counsel are still barristers.

Crown Court Appellate Functions

The Crown Court takes appeals on conviction or sentence from magistrates' courts. If the defence disputes the verdict of the justices or feels the sentence is too harsh, then an appeal may be made accordingly. During appeals against conviction the case is heard again with witnesses present and subsequent cross-examination where necessary but there is no jury. If the appeal is against sentence only, then usually just the facts of the case are read in court. In all appeal cases the judges are assisted by up to four lay magistrates, who collectively decide whether to confirm, reverse or vary the original decision. This includes the power to increase the original sentence, provided it does not exceed the maximum sentencing powers that magistrates would hold in such cases. The Crown Court also has appellate jurisdiction in administrative matters such as betting, gaming and liquor licensing.

The most famous of all the Crown Courts is the Central Criminal Court in London, more commonly known as the Old Bailey. Generally, only the most serious or difficult criminal trials are held there. The diagram in Figure 4 provides a simplified illustration of the layout of a typical Crown Court.

3

The Civil Courts

Whereas criminal law is concerned with the state taking action against those who offend against society or the criminal code, civil law is a matter of individuals taking action against other individuals. The common link between criminal and civil law is that they are both concerned with the regulation of human conduct with the ultimate purpose of maintaining order in society. Most people are aware of those actions that constitute a crime. Civil law also covers an extremely wide range of human conduct, which includes breaches of contract, negligence, trespass, libel, divorce, probate, and many more. There are occasions when both criminal and civil law overlap. For instance, if a person hits another who sustains a severe bruise, the offender can expect to be prosecuted for the criminal offence of assault occasioning actual bodily harm and may also be liable for the civil wrong of assault and battery under an action for trespass to the person. In such cases, the victim is usually content to see the assailant punished in the criminal courts, although the injured party may in certain circumstances still seek redress in the civil courts for damages. Therein lies a further difference between criminal and civil law – the former seeks to punish, whereas the latter seeks to recompense. Yet both can occur within the same court, for instance a criminal court may punish the offender and award compensation to the victim.

The two contestants in a criminal trial are the prosecution and the defence. In nearly all such proceedings the Crown, representing the state, constitutes the prosecution, hence the usual case heading of:

R (Regina – representing the prosecution)	–	v.	–	Smith (The defendant)	(1999) (The year of the case)

The two contestants in a civil trial are the plaintiff (the person bringing the action) and the defendant, therefore case headings read:

Smith (The plaintiff)	–	v.	–	Jones (The defendant)	(1999) (The year of the case)

Whereas the initial purpose of criminal proceedings is to ascertain whether the defendant is guilty or not guilty, in civil trials the court initially has to decide whether the defendant is liable, and this being the case the next step is to ascertain the appropriate remedy which is often an award of damages to the plaintiff or sometimes an injunction. A further distinction between criminal and civil law is the standard of proof required. In criminal law it is judged on the criteria of beyond reasonable doubt, whereas in civil proceedings it is decided on the balance of probabilities. The standard of proof in civil proceedings is therefore not so high as that found in the criminal courts, which explains why some actions may fail in the criminal courts but can succeed under a civil action.

THE COUNTY COURT

County courts in their present form originated in 1846 in response to the need for a relatively less expensive method of recovering debts and other civil matters previously dealt with by the superior courts. County courts are now to be found in every district in England and Wales. Their jurisdiction is both wide and varied, although certain monetary limits are generally set upon each subject area. Any action which exceeds these parameters must generally be heard in the High Court although the Courts and Legal Services Act 1990 has enabled increasing numbers of more expensive claims to be devolved to county court level. The following actions are among those that may be heard in the county court:

Contract

Breaches of contract can apply to a myriad of everyday business transactions, but more commonly to goods and services supplied but not paid for. The general limit in such cases heard before the county court is £25,000.

Tort

The term 'tort' means a civil wrong and gives rise to a variety of actions including negligence and personal injury claims. Again, the usual limit is £25,000. Actions under contract and tort account for more cases in the county courts than any other.

The county courts as a whole also hear actions for recovery of land, contentious probate (£30,000 limit), bankruptcy, the liquidation of companies, Admiralty proceedings (which includes damage involving ships), and equity proceedings. The latter is subject to a maximum of £30,000 and covers a number of matters, such as repossession of property, maintenance of young children and the dissolving of partnerships. The county court also has jurisdiction in other areas including consumer protection, landlord and tenant disputes and race relations and sex discrimination cases. All actions regarding divorce, separation and nullity of marriage must first be heard in the county court. If defended, the action is transferred to the High Court. County courts are empowered to issue a wide range of orders under the Domestic Violence and Matrimonial Proceedings Act 1976 designed to protect battered spouses and their children from violent partners. Many of these orders are very similar to those which magistrates are empowered to issue under the same circumstances, although a different statute is involved as will be examined later. As mentioned above, the Courts and Legal Services Act 1990 has enabled a transfer of business between the High Court and the county court. Increasingly, more cases which formerly fell exclusively within the jurisdiction of the High Court are being devolved to county court level. There are certain exceptions, however, such as cases involving sums over the general limits, complex areas of law and applications for judicial review.

The Legal Personnel of the County Court

Judges in the county court are circuit judges who rank equally with those who sit in the Crown Court. They are assisted by district judges (or their assistants or deputies) who are lawyers with a seven-year general qualification and these generally hear the less serious and contentious cases, although they also have a certain amount of concurrent jurisdiction with the circuit judges. It is usually the district judges who deal with cases in the small claims section of the county court, where a relatively quick and inexpensive arbitration procedure is used for claims not exceeding £3,000. District judges were formerly known as Registrars but were renamed by the Courts and Legal Services Act 1990.

THE HIGH COURT

The High Court of Justice has been widely featured in the media in recent years since a number of spectacular civil trials have occurred there involving important legal issues and well-known public figures.

The main centre of the High Court is located in the Royal Courts of Justice in the Strand in central London although there are a number of centres throughout England and Wales where the High Court may sit. This court has unlimited civil jurisdiction and performs an important appellate role in certain civil and criminal cases which will be mentioned later. Chapter 1 explained how a number of courts became fused into this single entity known as the High Court. In its modern form it now consists of three branches, namely the Chancery, Queen's Bench and Family Divisions.

The Chancery Division

The jurisdiction of this division covers such matters as

the sale of property, the administration of the estates of deceased persons and mental patients, contentious probate, deeds, trusts, company law, bankruptcy, revenue matters, partnerships and patents. About 13 judges preside over this court, headed nominally by the Lord Chancellor and assisted by the Vice Chancellor, who in practice is the one who oversees the overall function of this division. On occasions, the Chancery Division hears appeals from the county court on bankruptcy matters and also takes appeals from some tribunals.

The Queen's Bench Division

This division hears the more serious contract and tort actions which account for the bulk of its work. Since it now contains the old Admiralty Court, the Queen's Bench Division also deals with cases under maritime law and, since 1971, contains the Commercial Court. The most dynamically expanding area of law under the jurisdiction of the Queen's Bench Division comes under the heading of judicial review, which is an aspect of administrative law. This important area of law is concerned with actions brought by individuals against public authorities who exceed, abuse or fail to use their powers. This applies to local authorities, government ministers and the 'inferior courts' which include magistrates' courts and tribunals. The main purpose of applications for judicial review is to obtain one or more of the prerogative orders of *mandamus, certiorari* and *prohibition* which are not available to courts lower than the High Court.

The appellate jurisdiction of the Queen's Bench Division covers appeals on points of law from the Crown Court and criminal proceedings in magistrates' courts by way of 'case stated', meaning that the defence or prosecution disputes a decision on the grounds of interpretation of the law, rather than on the facts of the case. The Queen's Bench Division also has appellate jurisdiction over certain tribunals. Whenever two or more judges from this division sit together it becomes the Divisional Court of the Queen's Bench Division, which usually applies when it hears appeals or deals with judicial review cases. This court is headed by the Lord Chief Justice who is assisted by approximately 53 judges.

The Family Division

The work of this division of the High Court is almost self-explanatory, since it deals with the more serious and contentious domestic and matrimonial proceedings. These include matters of child custody, wardship, guardianship, adoption and maintenance, in addition to hearing defended divorces. It also takes appeals from magistrates' courts on domestic cases within their jurisdiction. The head of the Family Division is known as the President and is assisted by approximately 18 judges.

THE LEGAL PERSONNEL OF THE HIGH COURT

All of the judges (there are approximately 90 or more) in the High Court are known as 'puisne' judges (pronounced 'puny') and on appointment are automatically given knighthoods or made dames. They often sit alone during proceedings and are addressed as 'My Lord' or My Lady' in court. Judges in the High Court are assisted by Masters and Registrars.

The Civil Jurisdiction of Magistrates' Courts

In addition to their very important role within the criminal justice system, magistrates' courts also have jurisdiction in a number of civil and administrative proceedings. In the latter context they deal with betting, gaming and liquor licences, and in civil proceedings they have jurisdiction over the payment of income tax, local rates, water, gas and electricity, plus wide powers under domestic proceedings which include maintenance, adoption, guardianship and local authority care orders. As mentioned earlier, magistrates' courts have similar powers as the county court to issue orders for the protection of battered spouses and their children. In this instance these powers are exercised under the Domestic Proceedings and Magistrates' Courts Act 1978. When dealing with family law matters, a special panel of justices are used who constitute the 'family proceedings court'.

JURIES IN CIVIL PROCEEDINGS

The use of juries in civil cases is now relatively rare. While in theory, subject to the approval of the court, any civil case may be tried by a jury, in practice only four types of civil action may be subject to a jury decision, namely defamation, malicious prosecution, false imprisonment and fraud. Even then the court may waive this right if it is believed that the case may be too prolonged or technical. As will be examined later, juries are occasionally used in the Coroner's Court.

Much concern has been expressed in recent years regarding the relevance of juries in modern times. Some argue that they remain the last bastion of the common man's views against the perceived harshness and absurdity of certain aspects of the law, whereas others assert that they are inadequate in producing consistent justice. Particular concern is centred around serious fraud cases, where it is strongly argued that lay jurors are totally unsuited to reach verdicts on such highly technical matters. It has, therefore, been proposed that lay jurors in such cases should be replaced by panels of experts. Juries in certain defamation cases tried before the High Court have also been criticised for awarding excessively high damages. Consequently it seems likely that major reforms of the jury system may well occur in the not too distant future.

4

The Appellate Courts

In England and Wales we have the unique feature of a two-tier system of courts whose sole function is to hear appeals, namely the Court of Appeal and the House of Lords. The Court of Appeal is divided into two parts, the Civil Division and the Criminal Division, whereas the House of Lords takes on a more monolithic form and, subject to certain preconditions, hears both civil and criminal appeals.

THE COURT OF APPEAL (CIVIL DIVISION)

In most cases, appeals against county court judgments are directed to the Civil Division of the Court of Appeal. Exceptions to this general rule include bankruptcy appeals and a few other exceptions as laid down in Act of Parliament. Appeals are also taken from the High Court, subject to similar preclusions. Usually, three judges preside over each case and the outcome rests on a majority decision. During the hearing the main participants are the judges and the barristers representing each party. In this instance, they represent the appellant (the person appealing) and the respondent (the individual opposing the appeal).

Appeals are based either on a disputed verdict or the award of damages (or other remedy such as the terms of an injunction). The judges may therefore reverse, confirm or amend the decision taken in the previous court. Sometimes a retrial may be ordered depending on, for instance, new evidence coming to light or knowledge that one of the witnesses may not have told the truth. Witnesses are rarely called upon to participate in Court of Appeal proceedings since cases are usually decided on documentary evidence argued by the barristers before the judges. The head of the Civil Division of the Court of Appeal is known as the Master of the Rolls.

THE COURT OF APPEAL (CRIMINAL DIVISION)

This court hears appeals against criminal convictions or sentences from the Crown Court. If the matter disputed involves a question of law or fact, the Crown Court which originally tried the case must issue a certificate, or alternatively the Court of Appeal must give leave for an appeal hearing. Judges in the Court of Appeal may confirm, reverse or vary the original decision. In exceptional cases the original sentence can be increased, but not by the Court of Appeal of its own volition arising from an appeal by the appellant. This may only be considered on the application of the Attorney-General, generally where the more serious crimes are involved, particularly those involving violence, and where unreasonably lenient sentences have been given. The Attorney-General may make another form of reference to the Court of Appeal, where a defendant has been acquitted in the Crown Court on the basis of an unclear point of law contained in a trial judge's summing-up. Whatever the decision of the Court of Appeal, it cannot overturn the original jury verdict but makes a judgment which effectively clarifies the law for use in future cases.

The Attorney-General, therefore, plays an important part within the criminal justice system since he is one of the Law Officers of the Crown and the guardian of the public interest. Holders of this office are senior barristers and Members of Parliament within the majority party, and also act in the capacity as chief legal adviser to the government. The Attorney-General's numerous duties include the selection and supervision of the Director of Public Prosecutions who is responsible for the Crown Prosecution Service. The other Law Officer of the Crown is the Solicitor-General who, in essence, deputises for the Attorney-General.

A successful appeal against conviction means that the original conviction is 'quashed' on the grounds that it is unsafe thus rendering the original conviction void. Under certain circumstances, including the emergence of new evidence, a retrial may be ordered.[1] The head of the Criminal Division of the Court of Appeal is the Lord Chief Justice. A total of approximately 32 Lord Justices of Appeal constitute the main judicial presence in both divisions of the Court of Appeal. Sometimes High Court judges may sit in the Court of Appeal and it is common for two of these to preside exclusively over appeals against sentence. The Criminal Justice and Public Order Act 1994 enables specially selected circuit judges to decide criminal appeals, except where a High Court judge presided over the original case.

1. Under the Criminal Procedure and Investigations Act 1996, persons acquitted of an offence may be re-tried if they have since been convicted of an offence involving interfering with or intimidating jurors or witnesses in the earlier case. Such cases are known as 'tainted acquittals'.

THE CRIMINAL CASES REVIEW COMMISSION

The Criminal Appeal Act 1995 makes provision for the formation of the Criminal Cases Review Commission which is intended to take effect during 1996. The purpose behind the creation of this new body is to alleviate miscarriages of justice. The Commission will consist of 11 members who can be asked by the Court of Appeal to investigate specific cases. The Commission may also, on behalf of appellants, refer appeals against conviction or sentence to the Court of Appeal (except mandatory life imprisonment), or to the Crown Court where appropriate.

THE HOUSE OF LORDS

The House of Lords, situated within the Houses of Parliament, has a two-fold purpose. First, it constitutes the upper chamber of our legislature and, secondly, it houses the highest appellate court in the land. Only cases involving important and complex points of law or those of major public interest are given leave to appeal to the House of Lords. The vast majority are referred from both divisions of the Court of Appeal, although on rare occasions they can be taken direct from the High Court. This is known as the 'leap-frog system'.

Until 1876 it was possible for any Peer eligible to sit in the House of Lords, whether legally educated or not, to participate in appeal proceedings. Since then the present system has evolved, whereby the Lord Chancellor and up to 11 Lords of Appeal in Ordinary (the 'Law Lords'), hear appeal cases brought before them. The Law Lords usually sit in groups of five (the most important cases usually consist of seven or more) and conduct proceedings not in a lofty court-room but in a committee room. Neither do they wear resplendent robes but instead are attired in lounge suits. The room in which they hear appeals contains no raised dias or witness stand, yet they are among the nation's most eminent judges. Proceedings consist of discussions between the Law Lords and the barristers representing both parties in a very sedate atmosphere. The outcome is decided on a simple majority and, in contrast to the other courts, judgments are called 'speeches' and are usually delivered in written form and read out in the main chamber of the House of Lords. Far more appeal cases are handled by the Court of Appeal as a whole than the House of Lords. In one year, approximately 9,000 cases were heard by the former compared to about 120 by the latter, giving weight to the argument that, in the everyday sense, the Court of Appeal is the more important of the two, although ultimately it is not the most powerful.

5

Other Courts

The main embodiment of courts within the English legal system has been covered but a number of other bodies exercising important jurisdiction have yet to be mentioned. These include the Judicial Committee of the Privy Council, the Coroner's Court and finally the European Court of Justice and the European Court of Human Rights. Although the last two are regarded as foreign courts, they are both having an increasing effect upon our domestic law, particularly the European Court of Justice.

THE JUDICIAL COMMITTEE OF THE PRIVY COUNCIL

At the height of Britain's colonial power, the Judicial Committee of the Privy Council exercised the highest appellate function over those nations that constituted its Empire. In modern times a number of remaining colonies and former British territories still use this court as their final avenue of appeal. These include Hong Kong, New Zealand, Singapore, Fiji, Mauritius, the Seychelles, the Gambia, the Channel Islands, and several Caribbean countries including Jamaica,

Trinidad and Tobago, Barbados and the Bahamas. The court is comprised almost entirely of Law Lords, with five usually sitting on any one case, although occasionally their numbers are augmented by senior judges from the Commonwealth. The majority of appeals brought before the Judicial Committee involve the civil law, although it still maintains a high degree of influence on criminal law matters within the Commonwealth as shown in the relatively recent case of *Pratt v. Attorney-General for Jamaica (1993)*. As a result of this appeal, the Judicial Committee saved two men from execution and substituted life sentences on the grounds that it was inhuman and degrading that they had each waited 15 years for sentence to be carried out. This decision also had an effect on over one hundred other prisoners who had been subjected to similar gross delays. In this appeal, seven judges sat to decide the case which took place in London (always the venue for such proceedings).

The Judicial Committee of the Privy Council also acts as an appeal court for a number of professional tribunals and in certain ecclesiastical and Admiralty matters.

THE CORONER'S COURT

The main purpose of this court is to conduct inquests into unusual or unnatural deaths in order to ascertain their causes which may include any of the following verdicts: death by accident; death by misadventure; death by suicide; death through lack of care; death by unlawful killing; or death from natural causes. If the cause of death is uncertain the coroner will record an open verdict. Sometimes, a jury of between seven to 11

University of Huddersfield
Library and Computing Services
Lending Services:01484 473830
24/7 Renewals:01484 472045

Renewed Items 18/03/2010 13:43
XXXXXX6017

Item Title	Due Date
Methodology for planning tec	16/04/2010
Secondary and higher secor	16/04/2010
* The framework of the Engl	16/04/2010
* Sourcebook on the English	16/04/2010
Understanding social policy	26/03/2010
Children and young people's	16/04/2010
Researching health : qualita	16/04/2010

Amount Outstanding: £0.40

* Renewed today
www.hud.ac.uk

persons may be summoned at the coroner's discretion to hear the more serious and contentious inquests and decide upon the cause of death accordingly. However, it is compulsory for juries to be convened where a death occurred in prison or police custody, or resulted from an injury caused by the police.

Coroner's Courts possess some characteristics not normally associated with other aspects of the English court system. For instance, the coroner's themselves are not always lawyers since they can be medical practitioners with at least five years' experience. Those who are members of the legal profession must be either solicitors or barristers with a minimum of five years' standing. Proceedings are conducted more as an investigation than a trial and many of the rules of evidence as applied in other courts are not as strictly adhered to. As an example, hearsay evidence may sometimes be admissible in the Coroner's Court (evidence which is not given in person by a witness) and the opinions of non-qualified persons may also be taken into account. The jurisdiction of the coroner also extends to investigating treasure trove and the causes of certain fires in London only. There can be no appeal against a coroner's verdict, although an application may be made for judicial review on such grounds as excess of jurisdiction, error of law or fraud.

THE EUROPEAN COURT OF JUSTICE (THE COURT OF JUSTICE OF THE EUROPEAN COMMUNITIES)

As a result of the increasing integration of the European Union, the European Court of Justice is becoming more of an integral part of our legal system, despite it being classed as a foreign court. Technically, two forms of judgment from this court are binding upon any nation within the European Union, namely enforcement proceedings (when the European Court directs a state to comply with an EU law that it has broken) and preliminary rulings (where the European Court gives judgment on questions of Community law). However, certain judgments have been met with defiance and delay and in these situations the ultimate solution lies in political negotiations effected through the other organs of power within the European Union. The structure of the European Court of Justice basically consists of 15 judges (one from each member state) who are assisted by nine Advocates-General. The Advocates-General are very influential, since it is their task to provide the court with a reasoned opinion on each case and the judges usually follow their submissions.

The judges are selected to serve a six-year renewable term, although they can be dismissed upon the unanimous agreement of the other judges and the Advocates-General. Furthermore, they can be selected from those who occupy eminent judicial posts within their respective states or from the ranks of prominent academics. This latter criteria reflects one of the many aspects of the Continental system of justice that is distinct from our own which will be examined in greater detail later.

The European Court of Justice also hears cases which constitute a form of judicial review of the legality or otherwise of the actions of the institutions of the Union, particularly the Commission. However, as a result of the Single European Act 1986, a new Court of First Instance was instituted in 1989 to relieve the European Court of Justice of some of its increasing workload. The Court of First Instance consists of 15 judges whose jurisdiction is mainly confined to competition law matters and employment-related disputes between staff working for the institutions of the Union and their employers. Appeals against Court of First Instance decisions on points of law only may be made to the European Court of Justice.

THE EUROPEAN COURT OF HUMAN RIGHTS

It is important to distinguish between the European Court of Justice and the European Court of Human Rights. The latter court functions under the auspices of the Council of Europe, which is an association of 25 states, including Britain, who in 1950 formulated the European Convention on Human Rights. In order to enforce the Convention two bodies were established – the European Commission on Human Rights and the European Court of Human Rights. Any alleged infringement of the Convention must first be referred to the Commission which attempts to resolve the matter at a relatively informal level. If that fails it resorts to a further set of procedures that are complex and time-consuming. However, most complaints are resolved at this level. The few complaints that reach the European Court of Human Rights are often years old and at the outset its judgments are not binding upon our domestic courts. Its findings can nevertheless be very persuasive and sometimes acts committed contrary to the Convention are rectified either in anticipation of the judgment or very soon afterwards. In the longer term, findings of the Court have been known to influence our domestic legislation and even the interpretation of statutes and the development of the common law.

6

The Legal Profession

In previous chapters the work and function of the main courts within our system of the administration of justice have been described, with passing reference to those who service their workings. This chapter will examine the role of the lawyers who participate in court proceedings (the judges will be discussed later). There are two branches of the legal profession, solicitors and barristers. Solicitors constitute the most well-known branch of the profession, largely because they exist in far greater numbers than barristers and are generally the most accessible to the public. A large proportion of solicitors work in practices located in town centres and the main thoroughfares of large cities. Virtually anyone may enter such premises and arrange to see a solicitor on any of the vast array of matters they are qualified to deal with. Most of these do not entail court proceedings at all, but when they do in most cases it depends upon the category of court involved as to whether the solicitor will actually advocate for the client.

At present, the majority of solicitors only have full rights of audience in the magistrates' and county courts, whereas barristers have rights of audience at all levels in the court structure including the House of

Lords. In cases involving the use of barristers, it is still the solicitors who do most of the preparatory work, although much paperwork is also incumbent upon the barristers, particularly with regard to the drafting of pleadings in the civil courts. Whereas solicitors are usually in direct contact with their clients, barristers largely are not since they generally work from Chambers in the Inns of Court and receive their instructions via the solicitors. Barristers with around ten to 15 years' experience may be eligible to 'take silk', which means promotion to Queen's Counsel. These are the senior members of the Bar who constitute about 20 per cent of those practising. It is they who play the leading role in the more serious civil and criminal cases, particularly in the higher courts. In such cases it is usual for a QC to be assisted by an ordinary barrister, referred to in this instance as a junior. Those who 'take silk' (the term is derived from the fact that QCs wear silk gowns) command higher fees and also have a better chance of achieving the higher judicial posts since nearly all High Court judges are chosen from Queen's Counsel. Currently, about 300 solicitors have been given full rights of audience in the Crown Court and High Court and may now apply to become Queen's Counsel.

BACKGROUND AND TRAINING

Despite a number of reforms in more recent years, it is still widely felt that those practising at the Bar constitute the social elite of the legal profession and on analysis it is easy to understand why. The usual point of entry is by achieving a good honours degree in Law and joining one of the four Inns of Court: Lincolns Inn,

Grays Inn, the Middle Temple and Inner Temple. The aspiring barrister then has to pass the Bar Vocational Course which is a course equivalent to a year's full-time study, and from there he or she has to serve a year as an unpaid trainee in Chambers under an experienced barrister. This is known as 'pupillage'. During the two years normally spent in training and studying in one of the Inns of Court, it is compulsory to attend a total of 18 dinners – a tradition dating back to the Elizabethan age. Pupils who qualify are then 'called to the Bar', but only a minority go on to practise in this capacity. This is largely because there is a general shortage of tenancies within Chambers and also because there is no guaranteed income since the barrister relies solely on fees. Unlike solicitors they are not allowed to form partnerships, although they may now join solicitors' firms. Furthermore, they cannot take direct steps to find work as do solicitors, nor even sue for unpaid fees, but are reliant on the work given them by the Clerk of their Chambers.

In contrast, the route to becoming a solicitor and practising in that capacity is far less hazardous to persons without independent means, although it takes a year longer. Once again the most common route is through gaining an honours degree in Law and then a year spent studying for the solicitors' professional examinations (the Legal Practice Course) followed by two years as a trainee solicitor (or 'articled clerk') learning the practical aspects of a solicitor's duties. During this training period the participant is paid a salary in contrast to pupillage which, although lasting only one year, is unpaid. Also, once fully qualified, new solicitors may often be able to continue working for the same practice in which they served their articles, and will be paid a regular salary commensurate with their new professional status. Failing that they may be able to acquire a suitable post within another practice. Eventually, they may progress to the point of becoming a Partner within the practice and be entitled to a share of the profits in addition to a regular salary. However, in recent years many solicitors' practices have experienced difficulty in surviving the current economic climate. A significant loss of business has been evident due to a number of factors, including a substantial reduction in the availability of legal aid and the loss of their conveyancing monopoly. As a result, there has been a considerable reduction in the number of vacancies for trainee solicitors, especially in certain areas, and many wishing to enter the profession are currently unable to proceed to this stage.

Similarly, large numbers of newly qualified barristers have been forced to abandon the Bar either through lack of places within the Inns of Court in which to practice or because of insufficient work and subsequent lack of income. However, in contrast to the risks, the financial rewards for the most successful can be extremely high. Leading QCs have been known to earn more than £1m in fees in one year.

Both the inequalities and anomalies inherent within our divided legal profession have not gone unnoticed. Recent moves, particularly as a result of the Courts and Legal Services Act 1990, could result in the amalgamation of certain aspects of the barristers and the solicitors branches. This is already apparent in the Lord Chancellor's recent decision to give a number of solicitors full rights of audience in the superior courts. However, the future for many within both branches of the legal profession remains uncertain, especially for those newly embarking upon their careers.

7

The Judiciary

A number of legal, social and political commentators throughout the years have propounded the view that quality of justice is often reflected in the background and selection of the judiciary. The routes to the various judicial posts in this country are numerous and the diagram in Figure 5 gives a general overview of the main paths. This chapter on the judiciary includes the following section covering the magistracy.

THE MAGISTRATES

Lay magistrates are appointed by the Lord Chancellor upon the recommendation of local committees. The qualities sought in a prospective Justice of the Peace are the general requirements that they must be of good character and possess understanding of the important work they are to undertake. Many JPs are invited to apply by the local committees based upon their own knowledge of the candidates. This could be viewed as either an effective safeguard in the selection of persons who perform a very important public duty or as nepotism. Either way, recent surveys have disclosed that nearly 85 per cent of lay magistrates come from professional and managerial occupational groups but, as mentioned in Chapter 2, this is often due to the nature of work which does not fall within this category. For instance, unskilled or semi-skilled workers would generally find it far more difficult to obtain regular time-off to attend court. Furthermore, they may feel that their chances of promotion could be jeopardised due to regular absence from work, or simply could not afford to lose part of a day's pay in order to sit as a JP since the loss of earnings allowance is below that of the average national wage.

There are a number of full-time, salaried stipendiary magistrates who are legally qualified. However, there are currently no more than about 100 of those compared to approximately 30,000 lay justices in England and Wales. Stipendiaries do play, nevertheless, an increasingly important part in the exercise of summary justice throughout the country, even in areas where they are not normally based. For instance, they are sometimes called upon to help clear backlogs of cases in areas outside their usual metropolitan districts. This is due to the speed with which stipendiary magistrates are generally associated since their legally qualified status and experience enables them to reach decisions fairly quickly. They are also called upon to deal with cases outside their area which are particularly contentious or complex.

CIRCUIT JUDGES

The Lord Chancellor is also responsible for appointing circuit judges who preside in the Crown and county courts. About 90 per cent of circuit judges are appointed from the ranks of practising barristers, the remainder are solicitors, and until recently this was the highest judicial post that solicitors could aspire to. Even those chosen from the Bar to become circuit judges rarely progress further since it is generally the middle-range barristers who occupy these posts. The situation now seems destined for substantial change since the recent promotion of a circuit judge to the High Court who was also a solicitor.

DISTRICT JUDGES

The Courts and Legal Services Act 1990 renamed 'registrars' in the county court as 'district judges'. Their overall duties can be simply described as assisting circuit judges in the county court by hearing cases and dealing with other matters that do not usually fall within their jurisdiction. However, the role of district judges is very important since they try cases involving sums of up to £5,000, as well as take charge of the arbitration proceedings in the small claims section of the county court. They also have significant jurisdiction under matrimonial law. District judges are appointed by the Lord Chancellor and must be either barristers or solicitors who have held a general qualification for at least seven years. They are eligible for promotion to circuit judge after three years.

RECORDERS

A number of part-time judges exist in the Crown Court who are called recorders or assistant recorders. They are either barristers or solicitors of at least ten years' standing who attend a certain number of days in court in the capacity of judges presiding over the less serious criminal trials. Very often these part-time judicial posts are used as testing grounds for possible promotion to circuit judge or, in the case of very promising barristers (or even solicitors in the future), it may be used to prove their eligibility for appointment as judges to the High Court.

HIGH COURT JUDGES

The judges of the High Court are appointed by the Lord Chancellor usually from the ranks of QCs and with at least ten years' experience. The exact criteria for selection is not firmly established, except that the Lord Chancellor relies on a network of information gained from such sources as judges and senior barristers who are in a position to form an opinion about the candidate's suitability. As mentioned above, more circuit judges who display particular excellence in their duties may be promoted to the High Court Bench in the future.

COURT OF APPEAL JUDGES

The approximately 32 Lord Justices of Appeal are selected from the most accomplished of the High Court judges. It is the judges in both divisions – Civil and Criminal – of the Court of Appeal who principally shape the common law of this country, for it is they who preside over the bulk of major appeal cases and thus establish most of the legal precedents that are binding on all courts below them.

University of Huddersfield
Library and Computing Services
Lending Services 01484 473830
24/7 Renewals 01484 472045

Borrowed Items 03/03/2010 13:31
XXXXXX6017

Item Title	Due Date
Secondary and higher secor	15/03/2010
The framework of the Englis	17/03/2010
The driving instructor's guide	04/03/2010
English legal system in conte	17/03/2010
Sourcebook on the English l	17/03/2010
Economics for business	16/03/2010
Economics workbook	16/03/2010
English legal system : essen	17/03/2010

www.hud.ac.uk

THE LAW LORDS

The Lords of Appeal in Ordinary participate in the highest appellate court in the land, namely the House of Lords. They also constitute the main body of judges on the Judicial Committee of the Privy Council which is the highest court for a number of colonial states and former British territories. The Law Lords number between nine and 11 and may be augmented by the Lord Chancellor or any previous holder of that post. Usually two senior Scottish judges are included in their number. They generally sit in groups of five when hearing appeals, but occasionally seven or more may assemble if the case is particularly serious. The Law Lords are usually appointed from the Court of Appeal and automatically receive a life peerage which also entitles them to sit in the debating chamber of the House of Lords. However, it is a fundamental principle within our constitution that the judiciary must be separate from the legislature, therefore by custom and tradition the Law Lords usually speak in the debating chamber only on matters affecting the administration of justice. Only cases of major public concern or those involving important legal issues are given leave to appeal to the House of Lords. Although their judgments are binding upon all courts below them, including the Court of Appeal, they are not bound by their own earlier decisions and since 1966 they can depart from them. This is essential if the highest appellate court is to effect future judgments that reflect major changes in society. It must therefore be allowed to override its own previous decisions.

THE THREE MOST SENIOR JUDGES

The Lord Chancellor is commonly regarded as the head of the judiciary, although there are many other duties vested in this position of a judicial, administrative and legislative nature. In theory he is the head of the Chancery Division of the High Court, although in practice it is the Vice-Chancellor who carries out this task. Usually, a Lord Chancellor confines his judicial role to participating in appeals in the House of Lords or the Judicial Committee of the Privy Council, and even then such attendances are rare by virtue of the numerous other tasks he has to perform. These include responsibility for recommending and selecting all judicial appointees and the overall administration of such bodies as the Land Registry, the Public Records Office and the legal aid and advice schemes. It is important to note that the Lord Chancellor is a political appointee and that his position is not of a permanent nature since a change of government or even dismissal by a Prime Minister can cause his replacement. The political nature of this appointment is reflected in the fact that the Lord Chancellor is also a Cabinet Minister and Speaker of the House of Lords. In essence, he is regarded as the Minister for Justice, although the post is not formally categorised as such in this country.

The most senior permanent career judge is the Lord Chief Justice who only ranks below the Lord Chancellor. In addition to heading the Criminal Division of the Court of Appeal, he is also President of the Queen's Bench Division of the High Court. All holders of this office are automatically given life peerages. Next in the judicial hierarchy is the Master of the Rolls, who is head of the Civil Division of the Court of Appeal. The office-holder is in a position to play a leading part in shaping the development of the civil law and is thus included in the top three judicial appointments. The Master of the Rolls is also given a life peerage. It is ironic, however, that the Lord Chief Justice and the Master of the Rolls, while acknowledged as the most senior permanent career judges, are not allowed to take part in the appellate function of the House of Lords.

8

How The Judges Make and Interpret The Law

JUDICIAL PRECEDENT

It is essential to have both consistency in making legal judgments and the means to change them should such decisions fail to provide just solutions in an ever-changing society. This constitutes one of the main functions of the superior courts. Precedent is also an essential safeguard against the notion that judges make arbitrary decisions: like cases are decided alike, thus providing parties with some degree of certainty regarding the outcome of a proposed case. It is, therefore, the *general* rule that judges will follow judgments made in earlier cases that are sufficiently similar to cases brought before them unless there are very good reasons to disagree.

There are two categories of precedent, namely those which are 'persuasive' and those which are 'binding'. In essence, all precedents can be persuasive in varying degrees, whereas not all are binding. This falls under the doctrine of *stare decisis* which is fundamental to the operation of the common law and means 'let the decision stand'. The decision in an earlier case will be binding upon any later case if: (1) it contains a statement of law; (2) it forms part of the *ratio decidendi* of the later case (*ratio decidendi* means the grounds upon which an earlier decision was based); (3) it was decided by a superior court whose decisions are binding upon the court dealing with the later case; and (4) it does not contain any significant difference to the later case.

Sometimes judges may make a proposition of law which is not specifically directed towards the final judgment. This is called the *obiter dictum*, meaning words said in passing or by the way.

It is the *general* rule that decisions made in higher courts are binding upon courts below them and to a certain extent in courts at the same level. The way in which judicial precedent works is described as follows:

Magistrates' and County Courts

These courts are bound by decisions of the High Court, the Court of Appeal and the House of Lords. Magistrates' and County Courts are not bound by their own decisions, neither do they bind any other court, although they are expected to exercise consistent decision-making.

The Crown Court

This court is bound by decisions of the Court of Appeal and the House of Lords. Its decisions are generally regarded as persuasive, including those made by High Court judges sitting in the Crown Court.

The High Court

The decisions of this court are binding upon all inferior courts but not upon other High Court judges, although in practice they rarely go against each other's decisions. High Court decisions are not binding upon the Divisional Court (where two or more High Court judges sit together). All Court of Appeal and House of Lords' decisions are binding upon the High Court.

The Divisional Court

The decisions of the Divisional Court are binding upon High Court judges sitting alone and also the inferior courts except the Employment Appeal Tribunal. The Divisional Court is bound by the Court of Appeal and the House of Lords, and also by its own decisions.

The Court of Appeal (Civil Division)

Generally, its decisions are binding upon the Divisional Court, individual High Court judges and the inferior courts, including the Employment Appeal Tribunal. It must follow decisions of the House of Lords. In *Young v. Bristol Aeroplane Co Ltd (1944)* it was held that the Court of Appeal is bound by its own decisions unless: (1) it is a Court of Appeal decision given *per incuriam* (the omission of a very important component which subsequently flaws the decision); (2) where it involves an earlier conflicting decision by the Court of Appeal, it may then choose which case to follow; and (3) where an earlier Court of Appeal decision cannot stand with a later House of Lords' decision even though it did not expressly overrule it.

The Court of Appeal (Criminal Division)

This appellate court is bound by House of Lords' decisions and is generally bound by its own decisions but not so rigidly as in the Civil Division since the liberty of the appellant is often at stake.

The House of Lords

Since 1966 the House of Lords need no longer be bound by its own decisions, although it was stated in the Practice Statement (Judicial Procedure) 1966 that this rule should be used cautiously, especially in property and taxation matters and also the criminal law. Great weight is attached to statements made in the House of Lords even when they are said in *obiter*. Any House of Lords' decision can be overridden by Act of Parliament.

Precedents in other courts may be persuasive depending upon the status of the court, the reputation of the judge and the country in which it was established.

THE MECHANISM OF JUDICIAL PRECEDENT

Distinguishing a Case

This occurs where a court has been invited to follow a previous decision but feels there are important points of difference between that earlier decision and the case on which it was based, and the case now before it. This applies to both binding and persuasive precedent.

Following a Previous Decision

In effect this is the reverse of distinguishing a case.

Overruling a Decision

An earlier decision may be overruled by statute or by a

higher court. In the latter instance the overruling operates retrospectively, whereas if done by statute it usually takes effect on an effective date in the future. Once overruled, the case loses its authority.

STATUTORY INTERPRETATION

Words can have many different meanings – even the simplest of phrases can be interpreted in a variety of ways. For instance, a man says to his chauffeur 'Drive me to the station'. The driver will then be confronted with a number of problems, such as: (1) does he want to go to the station now or later? (2) which station? (3) in what car should he be taken? (4) does he want to take anything with him? The same basic problem confronts judges when interpreting Acts of Parliament.

Lord Hailsham once said that about 90 per cent of cases heard in the Court of Appeal and the House of Lords involved the meaning of words contained within statutes or delegated legislation. A major problem entailed in formulating legislation is that the lawyers who draft Parliamentary Bills work under great pressure of time. Also, in order to avoid creating too much opposition, they use language which must be 'flat' in style and which is often verbose. An example of how words in a statute can be interpreted in a variety of ways can be seen in the offence of burglary under the Theft Act 1968, where a person who enters a 'building' as a trespasser, in order to commit theft or certain other offences, is guilty of burglary. The word 'building' has been subsequently interpreted by the courts over the years as being a houseboat, a caravan and even a large commercial refrigerator, in addition to houses, ware-houses, factories and shops. Such problems often occur because Parliamentary draftsmen frequently have to draw up draft Bills for the future and are, therefore, unable to foresee every eventuality. However, the greatest single factor which causes multiple interpretations of words contained within statutes is that many Bills are worded in such a manner in order to try to appease a number of competing factions.

THE THREE RULES OF STATUTORY INTERPRETATION

The Literal Rule

This means that the courts use the literal meaning of words in a statute even if an absurd result occurs. In 1892 Lord Esher said that if the words of a statute were clear, they must be followed even if the result is not sensible. He went on to say that it had nothing to do with the courts if Parliament had caused such an absurdity. In 1884 Lord Bramwell said that if Parliament created such absurdities then it was the job of Parliament to alter the words and not the courts.

The Golden Rule

This interpretation was first used in 1854 in the case of *Mattison v. Hart*. It means that if the words of a statute in terms of their ordinary meaning produce an absurd result, these words may be modified in order to avoid the absurdity but it must not be taken beyond that. In other words the literal approach should be followed until it produces an absurdity, in which case the court should find some other meaning. The Golden Rule is based on the narrow interpretation of certain words and excludes surrounding circumstances.

The Mischief Rule

This is defined in *Heydon's Case (1584)*, where four points were considered, namely: (1) What was the common law before the relevant Act of Parliament was passed? (2) What was the 'mischief' (or defect) that the common law did not rectify? (3) What remedy did Parliament set out to achieve? (4) Why did Parliament set out to achieve this remedy? The courts should then endeavour to rectify the 'mischief' or defect.

ANALYSIS OF THE THREE RULES

The Literal Rule is the most widely used by the judges. In support of this, Lord Brougham said, in 1840, that if the courts departed from interpreting Acts using the ordinary meaning of their wording, they were effectively altering those Acts and were thus making law. He went on to say that this would be justifiable when dealing with ancient statutes since they were extremely concise, but this was not justifiable when dealing with modern statutes which are more detailed. In *Magor & St Mellons Rural District Council v. Newport Corporation (1952)*, Lord Simonds said that if a gap is evident within a statute, the solution lies in amending that Act and it would be most improper for judges to guess what Parliament would have done if that gap had been discovered by them. This would be tantamount to the courts usurping the Legislature.

Criticisms of the Literal Rule

(1) Words taken in isolation may have different meanings when used in sentences or paragraphs.

(2) If a dictionary is used it will often give more than one meaning of a word.

(3) General words can also have several meanings.

(4) Even if the meaning of a word seems plain, the judges may still disagree as to its interpretation because each may have different views regarding what the plain meaning is.

(5) In court proceedings there are two parties. Each may put forward a different meaning to one or more words. Out of the two, who is right?

It has been suggested that the Literal approach to statutory interpretation is not to be construed as the judiciary bowing before the sovereignty of Parliament, but is due largely to their belief, originating in ancient times, that the common law is superior in form to statutes. In effect, the judges blame Parliament for any absurdities in the law produced as a result.

In *Whiteley v. Chappell (1868)*, an Act of Parliament made it an offence for anyone during an election to impersonate another person who was entitled to vote. The defendant in this case impersonated a dead person under these circumstances. The court used the narrow Literal Rule and ruled that a person entitled to vote can only mean a person so entitled at the time and that the statute did not mention impersonating anyone who was dead. The judges therefore held that no offence had been committed.

The Literal Rule continues to flourish as seen in *Griffith v. Secretary of State for the Environment (1983)*, where the plaintiff had six weeks to appeal against the Secretary of State's refusal to grant planning permission. The House of Lords held that action was taken as soon as a civil servant had date stamped the decision even though the letter was never sent.

The Golden Rule, according to Professor Michael Zander (1993), is also unsatisfactory because it relies on the Literal Rule being applied first, and only when it leads to an absurdity will the Golden Rule be used. But what constitutes an absurdity? Different courts may or may not hold that an absurd result has occurred. Furthermore, there are no set guidelines as to when the Literal Rule ends and the Golden Rule begins. Professor Zander goes on to say that the Golden Rule is '...little more than an unpredictable safety-valve to permit the courts to escape from some of the more unpalatable effects of the Literal Rule'.

Professor Zander believes that the Mischief Rule is a great improvement on the other two since the court takes into account the context in which doubtful words or phrases appear, and therefore the court goes beyond those actual words or phrases. In doing so, the court considers why the statute was passed and interprets its wording accordingly. But where can this purpose or intention be discovered? In 1975, Lord Diplock said that older statutes had long preambles which stated the 'mischief' they were intending to remedy, whereas modern Acts do not usually have this.

Until recently, a major problem with the Mischief Rule was that judges were strictly prohibited from looking beyond the statute. However, this strict rule has been gradually relaxed, especially in more recent years. Some relaxation of this strict rule occurred in the nineteenth century when it became permissible to examine the 'long' and the 'short' title of a statute and for the courts to look at any preamble. Marginal notes which summarise certain points may also be examined, although this is frowned upon since they are not inserted by Parliament. Headings to sections and schedules may additionally be used in construing an Act of Parliament. Punctuation marks can also be used, although this only applies to modern statutes since older Acts contained few, if any, of these. Earlier statutes containing the same subject-matter may be consulted in order to trace the history of a particular phrase. In such instances the court will presume that Parliament was influenced by earlier legislation.

EVIDENCE BEYOND JUDICIAL DECISIONS AND STATUTES (EXTRINSIC OR EXTERNAL AIDS)

In 1957 Lord Simonds said that he felt it was his right and duty not only to examine every part of a statute but also to explore every 'other legitimate means'. It was suggested here that the search for the meaning of a phrase could extend beyond the statute itself, other statutes and legal precedents (the common law). Various sources of extrinsic materials include the following:

(1) Historical Background

The courts are always willing to hear counsel state the historical background of a statute but *only* if earlier cases or *legal* textbooks are used. Note that only legal sources are permissible and not other textbooks.

(2) Government Publications

Reports of various law reform committees, including Royal Commissions, can be used as well as those pertaining to the proceedings of other Parliamentary committees (since 1975) and also explanatory memoranda to Bills (since 1988).

(3) Parliamentary Debates

Until recently, the use of *Hansard* to interpret Statutes was strictly prohibited but this is now permissible where necessary in the light of the House of Lords' decision in *Pepper v. Hart (1993)*.

(4) International Treaties or Conventions

The courts may use these provided they form the basis of UK legislation.

In Britain we have had an Interpretation Act since 1889; a more recent version was enacted in 1978 but it is primarily intended to guide Parliamentary draftsmen. A number of other countries have gone beyond mere guidance to draftsmen and have attempted to guide their judges. In 1980 Lord Scarman made two attempts to put legislation through Parliament in order to provide the courts with a wider range of aids to interpret statutes but both failed.

There has been some criticism of the courts seeking out the intention of Parliament, since a small number of people actually draft statutes, relatively few speak on them during debates, many often vote against them, and even those who vote in their favour do not always know what they are voting for or are compelled to support them.

Although it is generally understood that statutes should be interpreted in the sense that they were written, they are often construed in accordance with modern trends, since certain words are 'fluid' in their meaning as, for instance, the word 'insulting'.

OUR MEMBERSHIP OF THE EUROPEAN UNION – HOW HAS IT AFFECTED STATUTORY INTERPRETATION?

In *HP Bulmer Ltd v. J. Bollinger S.A. (1974)*, Lord Denning MR said that the English Literal Rule is inadequate when interpreting the Treaty of Rome as, unlike our statutes, it is so broadly worded. As a result, the Treaty of Rome has to be clarified by secondary legislation, namely Directives, Regulations and Decisions, and also by the judges who fill-in the gaps. Lord Denning went on to say that the English system is also inadequate when interpreting secondary legislation since that too is often very broadly worded. English judges must, therefore, adopt the same procedures as the European Court of Justice as do judges in other states within the European Union, namely to look at the purpose or intent of such legislation.

In *Buchanan & Co Ltd v. Babco UK Ltd (1977)*, Lord Denning MR further commented that he had visited the European Court of Justice and discovered that they used the 'schematic' or 'teleological' system, meaning that they go by the design or purpose of the legislation and will fill-in any gaps without hesitation. This was virtually a hint at the House of Lords who earlier, in *Magor & St Mellons Rural District Council v. Newport Corporation (1952)*, had accused him of attempting to usurp the power of Parliament. Lord Denning added that when interpreting EC law it is essential that a wider form of interpretation is used.

This form of interpretation has been used several times in the English courts, such as in *Attorney-General's Reference (No.1 of 1988)*, when the Court of Appeal were asked to interpret the meaning of the word 'obtained' in respect of price-sensitive information used in earlier insider-dealing laws. The court ruled that this word meant 'receiving' or 'acquiring' through any means whatsoever, and that it did not only apply to persons making a positive effort to gain such information but also to those who were passive recipients. Here, the Court of Appeal examined the purpose of the Company Securities (Insider Dealing) Act 1985, which was intended to stop people taking advantage of privileged market information.

9

Court Proceedings – Enquiries or Contests?

The English system of trying cases in its courts comes under the heading of adversarial or accusatorial. This means that the court becomes the centre of a contest between both parties in which one emerges the winner. By the time of the trial each side should have gained as much information as possible to both support their own case as well as to exploit any weaknesses in the opposition's arguments. Once proceedings commence, particularly in criminal trials, the prosecution attempts to build a strong case against the defendant. The defence then endeavours to demolish the prosecution's case. Throughout this procedure witnesses are examined and cross-examined using a variety of tactics available to the skilled advocate. Some use subtle means to cause witnesses to react in a certain way, others use bullying tactics to obtain the same result from nervous participants. The success of a case, therefore, often rests upon the ability of an advocate to manipulate proceedings and not just the weight of evidence.

The adversarial system can often produce unexpected and, according to some observers, unjust results due to the manner in which evidence can be presented. The English system of justice, therefore, greatly hinges upon the events of the trial itself as much as the gathering of evidence beforehand, since the courts only judge what is presented before them and, especially when juries are present, the way it is presented. With the exception of the Coroner's Court, proceedings in the English courts do not constitute investigations into the matters brought before them, unlike the inquisitorial system adopted in many countries, including mainland Europe. This system basically entails an examining judge conducting his own investigation, often in conjunction with organisations such as the police, before any trial takes place. In effect this procedure is a search for the truth, taking into account all aspects of the matter, and consequently a substantial number of cases do not reach the trial stage. Those that do go to trial often reach that point with far greater certainty as to the outcome than in courts using the adversarial system.

According to Lord Lane CJ (1992) many of our advocates appearing for the first time before the European Court of Justice find enormous difficulty in adjusting to the European inquisitorial style of justice. But he goes on to state that, despite the advantages of this system, it is not a panacea and mentions that Germany is considering changing to the adversarial system in due course.

For all its complexities, anomalies and, at times, eccentricities, the English legal system has still been copied by many nations throughout the globe on an impressive scale. In fact, about a third of the world's population is ruled by laws and legal systems which originated in England. The fact that our present system is the result of nearly 1,000 years unbroken development may hold the answer to its general success, despite all arguments to the contrary. Such a system reflects the socio-economic as well as legal developments of this nation throughout this period which themselves have not progressed in straight lines – hence the convoluted structure of the English court system which assumes the shape of responsiveness. Perhaps the main source of current criticism regarding the English legal system is the time it takes to effect important changes, in which case it is the reform-making process which is at fault rather than the system it seeks to change.

FIGURE 1

THE STRUCTURE OF THE COURTS

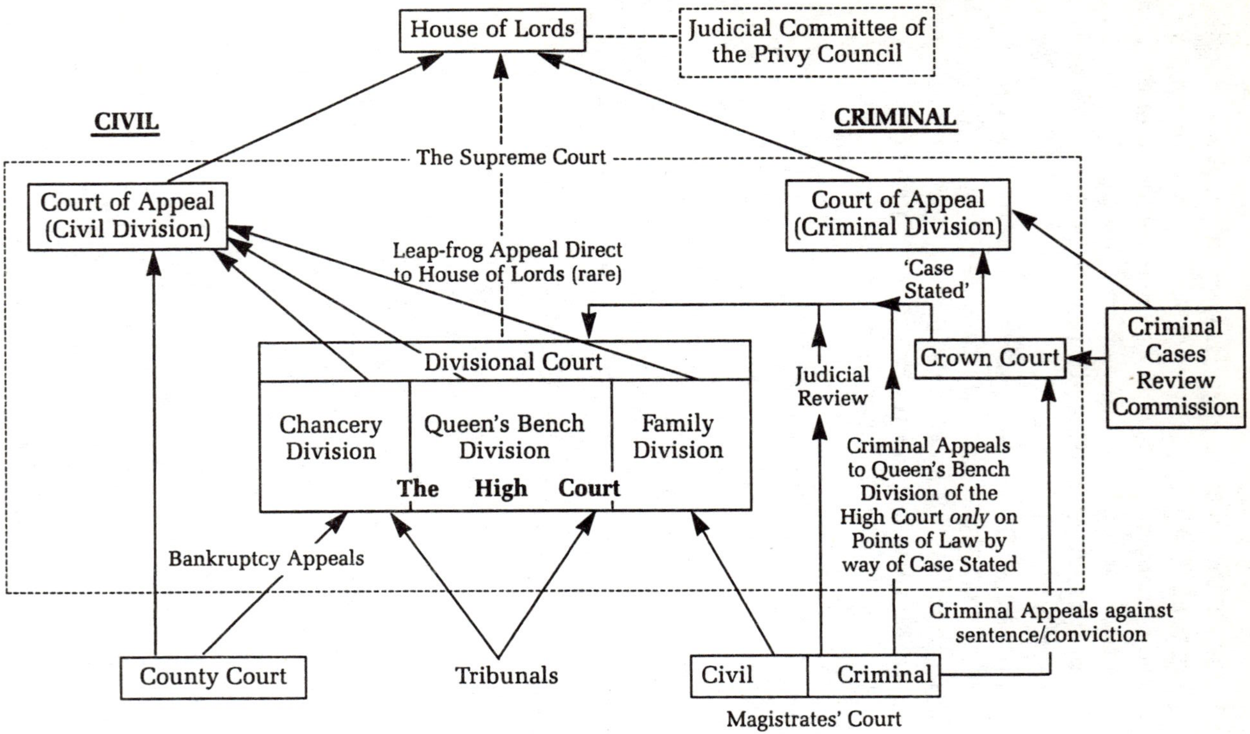

FIGURE 2

PASSAGE OF CRIMINAL OFFENCES THROUGH MAGISTRATES' COURTS

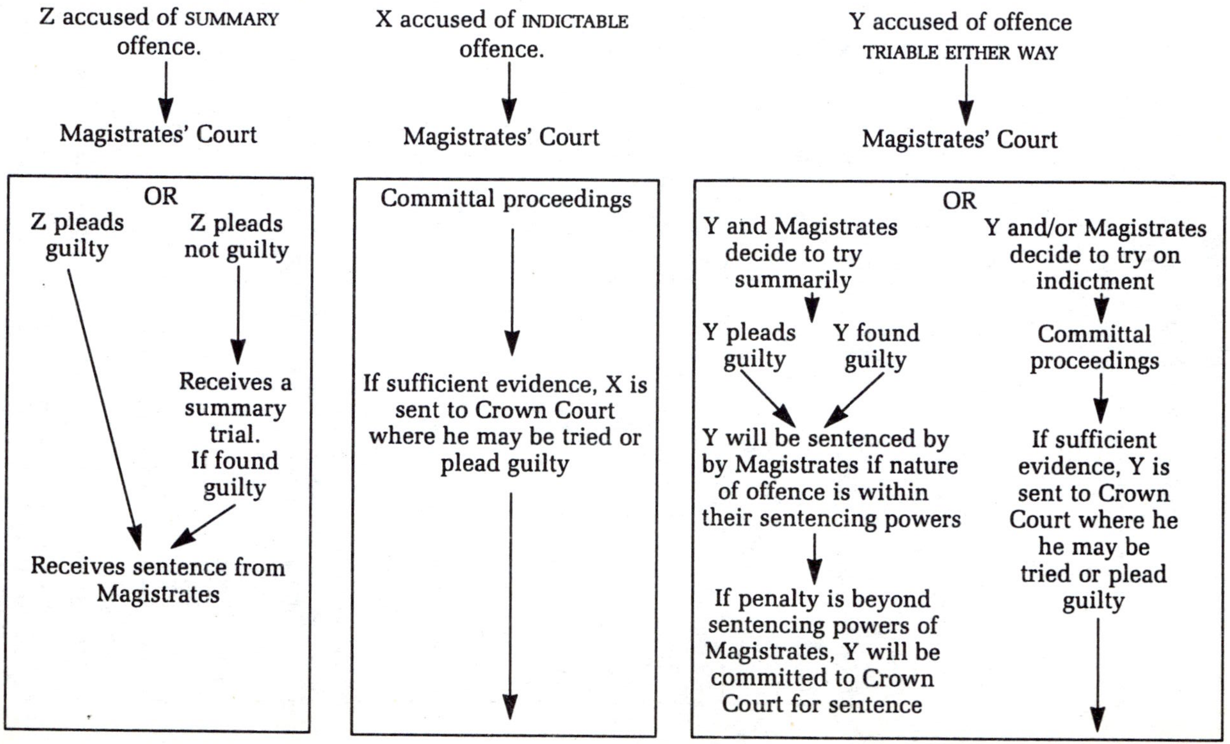

FIGURE 3

THE MAIN CRIMINAL SANCTIONS

AGE LAST BIRTHDAY

	Usually dealt with in the Youth Court							
PENALTY	**14**	**15**	**16**	**17**	**18**	**19**	**20**	**21**
Bind-overs (Offenders)*	●	●	●	●	●	●	●	●
Discharges*	●	●	●	●	●	●	●	●
Fines*	●	●	●	●	●	●	●	●
Compensation Orders*	●	●	●	●	●	●	●	●
Deprivation of Property (Forfeiture, Restitution and Confiscation Orders)*	●	●	●	●	●	●	●	●
Probation			●	●	●	●	●	●
Community Service			●	●	●	●	●	●
Combination Order			●	●	●	●	●	●
Curfew Order**			●	●	●	●	●	●
Supervision Order*	●	●	●	●				
Attendance Centre Order*	●	●	●	●	●	●	●	
Detention in Young Offender Institution		●	●	●	●	●	●	
Imprisonment								●
Detention during Her Majesty's pleasure*	●	●	●	●				
Life Sentence					●	●	●	●
Secure Training Order***	●							

* Also available for 10–13-year-olds (inclusive)

** Currently available in limited areas with electronic monitoring

*** Also available for 12 and 13-year-olds (inclusive) but not until 1996

FIGURE 4

A TYPICAL CROWN COURT

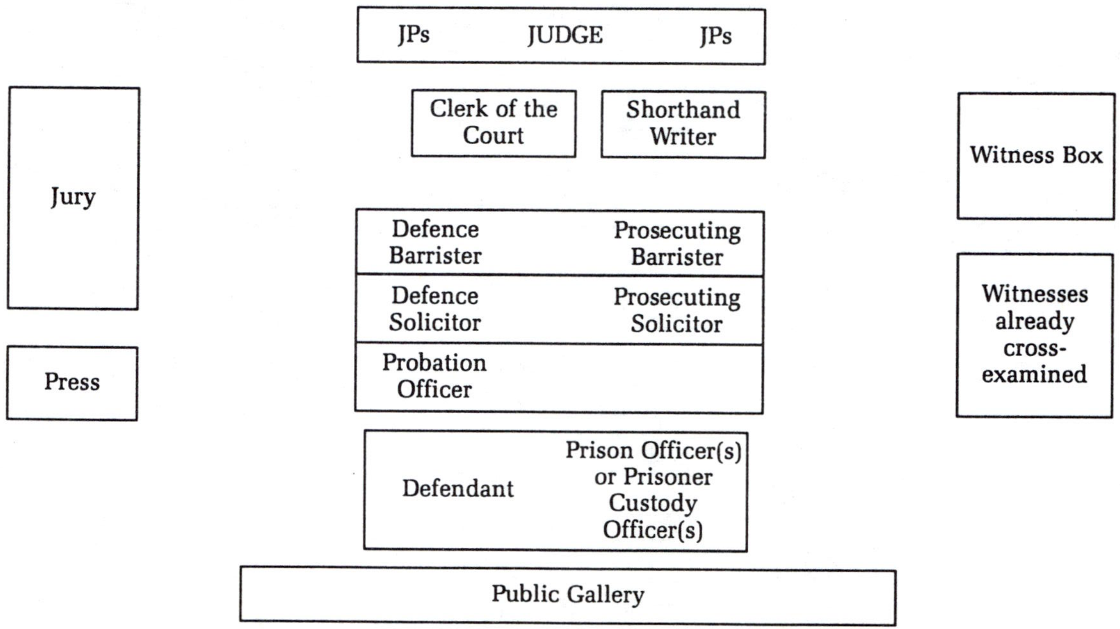

FIGURE 5

THE JUDICIAL PATH

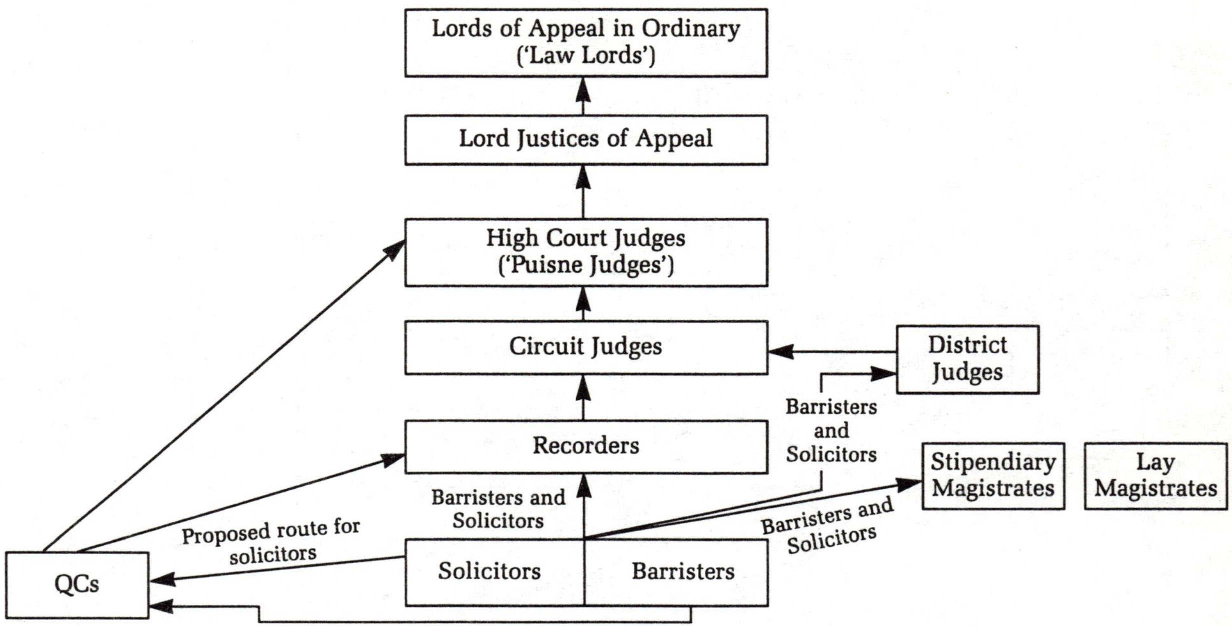

Recommended Further Reading

C. Elliott and F. Quinn, *English Legal System* (Longman, 1996).

T. Ingman, *The English Legal Process*, 6th edition (The Blackstone Press, 1996).

L. Jason-Lloyd, *The Framework of Criminal Law* (Frank Cass, 1996).

L. Jason-Lloyd, *The Legal Framework of the Constitution* (Frank Cass, 1996).

Ronald Walker and Richard Ward, *Walker and Walker's English Legal System*, 7th edition (Butterworths, 1994).

M. Zander, *Cases and Materials on the English Legal System*, 7th edition (Butterworths, 1996).

Index

Table of Statutes

Table of Cases